Tom and Ricky
and the
Gold Mine Mystery

Bob Wright

High Noon Books
No

Cover Design: Nancy Peach
Interior Illustrations: Herb Heidinger
Story: Helen Dressling Corliss

Glossary: minor, ore, blast, flashlight, battery, swimsuits, tunnel

International Standard Book Number: 0-87879-395-X

10 09 08 07 06 05 04 03
15 14 13 12 11 10 9 8 7

Contents

CHAPTER 1

Gold at the Creek?

It was Saturday morning. It was already a sunny day. Tom rode his bike over to his friend Ricky's house.

Ricky was sitting on the front steps. He was brushing Patches' coat. Patches wagged his tail.

Tom sat down on the steps. He said, "What do you want to do today? It's going to be warm."

"We could go swimming in the creek. Then we could go fishing," Ricky said.

Tom smiled. "That's a good idea."

Patches barked. He wanted to go, too.

Ricky's mom came out. She said, "Mr. Bell called. He has a hard time getting around. He needs some work done in his yard."

"Does he have much work to do?" Ricky asked.

Tom said, "We want to go out to the creek and swim."

Ricky's mom said, "Why don't you go over and talk to Mr. Bell?"

Ricky said, "That is a good idea. Let's go."

"OK," Tom said.

Mr. Bell was in his front yard. He lived near Ricky. He was old. Yard work was hard for him. He liked the boys and they liked him.

Ricky called out, "Hi, Mr. Bell. What work do you need done?"

Mr. Bell smiled. "I'm glad to see you boys. Could you pull weeds a few mornings this week? It gets too hot in the afternoon."

Ricky said, "Sure, we will be glad to pull weeds in the mornings. We want to swim this afternoon."

"Are you going to swim in the creek?" Mr. Bell asked.

"Yes. There's a good place there. Some big rocks form a nice pool," Tom said.

"I swam there when I was a little boy. My father worked in the old gold mine out past there," Mr. Bell said.

"Really? Is it still there?" Ricky asked.

Mr. Bell laughed. "Well, gold mines do not go away. That one had a cave-in."

"Mr. Bell, did your father get much gold?" Tom asked.

"No, I don't think so. That is partly why the men stopped mining. The gold gave out."

"How do you find the gold?" Ricky asked.

Mr. Bell said, "In this kind of mine the miners dig into a hill. They blast to break up the ore. After blasting, the ore is taken to a mill."

"I know. Gold is taken out of the ore at the mill," Ricky said.

"Sometimes people find gold in a river," Tom said.

"Yes, that is another kind of mining," Mr. Bell said.

"Maybe we will find gold in the creek," Ricky said.

"Wouldn't that be something if we did find gold in the creek?" Tom said.

"Yes, it would," Mr. Bell answered.

"Do you think we might?" Tom asked.

"If you did, you would start a gold rush," Mr. Bell answered.

"A gold rush? You mean that people would come from all over to find more gold?" Ricky asked.

"That's right. That's what would happen," Mr. Bell said.

"I don't think we would want that to happen," Ricky said.

"Well, I don't think it will happen. No one has found any gold yet in that creek. If someone had, we would have heard about it," Mr. Bell said.

"Oh, well. It was nice to think about," Tom said.

"Come on. Let's start to work. We can make some money by weeding," Ricky said.

CHAPTER 2

Flashlights and Batteries

The boys were happy. They could earn some money. Then they would still have time to go swimming.

Tom and Ricky worked hard. They wanted to do a good job for Mr. Bell.

Mr. Bell was happy with their work. He said, "You did good work. Here is your pay."

"Thank you, Mr. Bell." Tom said.

Then Ricky said, "My flashlight is worn out. Now I can buy a new one."

"You know what? I need a flashlight, too. Let's go buy flashlights right away," Tom said.

Tom and Ricky rode their bikes down to King's Market. They picked out the flashlights. Then they got batteries.

Tom and Ricky rode their bikes back to Ricky's house. Patches was glad to see them. Ricky's mother saw them come in the house. "What's going on?" she asked.

"Mr. Bell told us about an old gold mine. It's near the creek. We're going to go swimming. Then we're going to look at the old mine," Ricky said.

"Well, be careful. Don't go too far into it. It's old. It could fall down on you," she said.

Ricky said, "We'll take Patches with us."

"OK," she said.

Soon the three were off. The boys put their things in packs on their backs. They rode their bikes on the old road out of town.

At last they reached the swimming hole.

"Oh, that water looks good," Tom said.

"It sure does," Ricky said. He ran down to the creek. Tom was right in back of him.

They got into their swimsuits. Then they jumped into the creek.

Patches swam with them.

Ricky said, "Oh, that feels good."

"I'm cooled off," Tom said.

Then they got out of the water.

Tom said, "I told Eddie we were coming out here. He and Dave will come out later. Eddie has a computer class today."

Patches swam with them.

CHAPTER 3

A Tunnel in a Cave

Tom and Ricky sat under a tree. Then Tom said, "Let's walk to the end of the road."

"I don't think it is very far," Ricky said.

"Maybe Eddie and Dave will get here soon. Then we can swim with them," Tom said.

They walked down the road a long way.

Patches ran beside them. All of a sudden he took off away from the road.

Ricky yelled, "Look at Patches! Look at him run! He's chasing a rabbit."

Tom said, "Look at that rabbit run!"

The rabbit and dog ran into the trees at the base of a hill. The boys ran after them.

They couldn't see Patches.

Ricky called Patches. Tom called him, too.

"Where did he go?" Ricky asked.

"He must be around here somewhere," Tom said.

They heard a bark come from some bushes.

"There he is. He's in those bushes," Ricky said.

The boys pushed through the bushes.

There was a hole in the hill.

"Look at that," Tom said.

"It looks like a cave," Ricky said.

"We never saw that before," Tom said.

"The bushes were in the way," Ricky said.

"Let's go in the cave," Tom said.

There was a tunnel inside the cave. And there was Patches waiting for them in the tunnel.

"That is a tunnel cut in the rocks," Ricky said.

"And it goes way back," Tom said.

"It goes into the hill. But where does it go from there?" Ricky asked.

"Let's find out," Tom said.

The tunnel ahead of them was dark.

Farther along the tunnel got darker.

Ricky said, "It is too dark back there."

Tom said, "We can't go any farther."

"We bought new flashlights. We bought batteries. Now we need them. And where are they?" Ricky said.

Tom laughed. "They are back by the swimming hole."

"A lot of good they do us there," Ricky said.

"Let's go back where we can see better," Tom said.

"OK," Ricky said.

Ricky picked up Patches. "No chasing in here, Patches. You may get lost."

Tom said, "Come on. Let's go get our flashlights."

"Right. Then we can find out where the tunnel goes," Ricky said.

"Do you think we'll find anything in this cave?" Tom asked.

"I don't know. But it's funny," Ricky said.

"How's that?" Tom asked.

"We always come over to the creek. But we never saw this cave before," Ricky said.

They walked back out of the cave. Then they started back for their flashlights.

CHAPTER 4

A Pick-up Truck

Tom and Ricky ran back to the swimming hole. Patches ran along with them.

Ricky said, "Eddie and Dave should be here soon."

Tom said, "We may as well go swimming. We can wait for them while we swim."

Ricky said, "Then we can show them the cave Patches found."

"Patches found it all right," Tom said.

Just then they heard something.

"Look, there are two men in a truck. Do you see them? And there are boxes on the truck," Ricky said.

Tom said, "What are they doing out here? There isn't anything way out here."

Tom said, "What are they doing out here? There isn't anything way out here."

Ricky said, "And the road isn't very good. And then it ends. It does not even go anywhere."

Tom said, "It does come to our swimming hole. A lot of the kids don't even know about our swimming hole."

"The truck might turn around pretty soon," Ricky said.

"Then we will see them come back," Tom added.

They waited. The truck did not come back.

"What should we do?" Tom asked.

"I hear the truck. It is coming back," Tom said.

Ricky said, "Look! There were boxes on the truck. Now the boxes are gone!"

"They must have left the boxes back down the road somewhere," Tom said.

"Let's go find those boxes. What do you think is in them?" Ricky asked.

"I wish I knew," Tom said.

"I have not seen those men before. They don't live around here," Ricky said.

"I think I saw them in town this week," Tom said.

"What were they doing?" Ricky asked.

"I was talking to Sergeant Collins. The men walked into King's Market. Maybe to buy flashlights," Tom said.

"The better to see in caves?" Ricky asked.

Tom said, "You are very funny! Let's get dressed. We don't need to wait for Eddie and Dave."

Ricky said, "I wish we could write them a note."

"They will see our bikes and come look for us," Tom said.

Ricky said, "This time I'll hold Patches. We don't want him to run after another rabbit."

Tom said, "Let's make sure we take our flashlights. We can look in the cave."

The three of them started to walk down the old dirt road.

Tom looked down at the road.

"Look at the tire tracks in the dust! Let's find out where they go," Tom said.

Ricky put Patches down. They all started to run.

All of a sudden Ricky stopped. "Did you hear that? Could it be the truck again?"

"It sure sounds like one," Tom said.

"Come on. Let's hide," Ricky said.

"Why?" Tom asked.

"So they won't see us," Ricky said.

"Won't see us?" Tom asked.

"That's right. We want to find out what's going on," Ricky said.

"OK, OK. Where can we hide? We need to see what's up," Tom said.

"Let's hide in these bushes. They won't see us," Ricky said.

Patches started to bark. Ricky grabbed him.

They ran in back of some bushes. Ricky held Patches. The truck went by them. They saw the same two men in the truck. Tom and Ricky didn't move. They just sat in back of the bushes.

CHAPTER 5

Gun Shots

The boys sat and waited. They didn't want to move. They wanted to wait until the truck came back.

Then Tom jumped up. "What was that?" he yelled.

"I think it was a gun," Ricky said.

"What could they be doing?" Tom asked.

Just then there was another shot.

"That's two shots," Tom said.

There was another bang.

Ricky said, "That makes three shots."

After that they heard more gun shots.

"What is going on?" Tom asked.

Ricky said, "I wish they would stop."

Tom said, "If only Sergeant Collins would come along now."

"Or anybody," Ricky added.

Tom said, "Well, not just anybody. We don't want to see more men like them."

Ricky laughed, "That's for sure."

"Let's stay right here. This is a good place to hide. We can't be seen from the road," Tom said.

"That's a good idea," Ricky said.

Tom said, "I hope Patches doesn't bark. Those men can't be far up the road."

Then they heard the truck and saw it go down the road. They waited. Then they started to walk on the road again.

"Look. There is the cave Patches ran into," Tom said.

"And look. The tire tracks keep on going past here," Ricky said.

"Let's come back to the cave later. I want to see where the tire tracks go," Tom said.

Pretty soon the tire tracks turned and went off the road. Tom and Ricky turned off the road, too.

"It looks like the tracks go all the way up to the hill," Tom said.

"They stop behind the trees," Ricky said.

"Look! There's another cave. It has wood over the opening," Tom said.

"Wow! It's the opening to the old gold mine!" Ricky said.

Tom said, "I bet you are right. We found the old gold mine!"

Ricky went to the opening. "Look. This wood is old. We can push this open."

Tom said, "Come on. Let's both push."

The wood was old. It didn't take much to push it down.

The opening to the mine was big. They walked in. They turned on their flashlights. There were rail tracks in the floor.

Ricky said, "They were for mining cars."

They walked slowly down a long tunnel. Ricky was ahead. He said, "Look, here is another tunnel."

Patches led the way into the new tunnel. Before long it got wider. Tom said, "It's as wide as a room here."

They shined their flashlights around. Ricky said, "Look at these boxes. Those are the ones we saw on the truck!"

Some of the boxes were open. The boys looked in them.

Ricky said, "There are some guns in these boxes!"

"What did they shoot? Come on. Let's get out of here," Tom said.

"OK, pretty soon. Here is another tunnel. Let's just look in it. We might find out something about the place," Ricky said.

Ricky shined his flashlight around.
All of a sudden he yelled, "Gold! It's gold!"

They came to another room. Ricky shined his flashlight around. All of a sudden he yelled, "Gold! It's gold! It's here on the wall in the rocks."

Tom said, "That has got to be gold right here in the rock wall. It's in plain sight."

Just then Patches started to bark.

Ricky said, "I hear the truck coming back!"

CHAPTER 6

Trapped!

"We can't go out. We will have to hide. Which way shall we go?" Ricky asked.

Tom said, "Look, here is another tunnel. Let's go in it. We have to get away from these rooms."

The boys came across another room. Ricky said, "Look at all the old mining cars in here. We can hide behind the mining cars. I'll hold Patches."

"I think I hear those men," Ricky said.

Tom said, "Me, too. They are in the mine."

Ricky said, "Now they are closer. I can hear them talking."

Tom, Ricky, and Patches didn't move. The boys wanted to hear what the men said.

"Did you hear that? One man said something about selling mining rights," Ricky said to Tom.

"Mining rights? What do you mean?" Tom asked.

"They would let someone pay to dig in this mine. But they would still own the mine," Ricky answered.

"Why do they want to do that? They found more gold," Tom said.

Ricky said, "We saw the gold. We know it is here. They must be up to something."

"Maybe it isn't real gold," Tom said.

"I just hope they don't find us. I hope they don't come this way," Ricky said.

Then they heard something above them.

They shined their flashlights up.

Tom said, "Bats! There are bats up there. They are all asleep."

"They sleep in the day and go out at night," Ricky said.

Just then they heard something else. "Those men must have dropped something," Tom said.

Patches barked.

"Oh, no," Tom said.

A man yelled, "Someone is in here. It's those kids. Those kids with the dog down by the swimming hole."

"We will have to get them," the other man said.

"They must have seen the gold. We don't want anyone to know about it yet."

Tom and Ricky ran fast. They could hear the men running, too. They turned into many tunnels. At last they stopped.

Ricky said, "I don't hear the men coming after us any more."

Then one of the men said, "Let them go. They will have to come out sooner or later. We can just wait for them."

Tom and Ricky started to walk again. They moved away, back into the tunnel. "Look at this place," Tom said.

Tom said, "Oh, no! The mine is still caving in."

"It's full of big rocks," Ricky said.

Tom said, "This must be the cave-in Mr. Bell told us about."

Ricky said, "I hope it doesn't cave in any more. We're dead ducks if it does."

Some small rocks fell down.

Tom said, "Oh, no! The mine is still caving in. Let's get away from here."

"Now we are lost. We don't know how to get out of the mine," Ricky said.

Tom said, "We must keep moving. We must get away from the cave-in."

CHAPTER 7

How to Get Away

At last they stopped. Then they sat down next to a wall. Patches sat down next to them.

"We better turn off our flashlights to save the batteries," Ricky said.

"You're right," Tom said.

"Boy, it's dark in here," Tom said.

They sat. They didn't talk. They waited to see if the men would come this way.

Then Tom said, "I don't hear those men any more."

Ricky said, "Maybe we should try to get out of here."

"We might see those men," Tom said.

"Let's keep one flashlight turned on part of the time," Ricky said.

"That's a good idea. We need to save our batteries. We may be here a long time," Tom said.

Then they heard something above them.

Tom said, "It's the bats again! Look at them flying around. Why are they flying around now?"

Ricky said, "I know. It must be dark outside. They wake up then and go out for the night."

Tom said, "How do they find their way out?"

"I'm not sure, but they must know the way out. They can fly without hitting anything. Let's see where they go," Ricky said.

Tom said, "These tunnels are not the same. We came in through other tunnels."

Ricky said, "Look, there is a little light ahead. I hope it is a way out."

Tom said, "It is! It is! It's moonlight."

Soon they went out of the mine through a cave entrance. Ricky said, "Why, that is the cave that Patches found when he chased the rabbit."

Tom said, "That hidden cave is a secret way into the mine. And a way out."

They ran fast until they got to the swimming

hole. They could see lights and cars there.

Ricky said, "That's my Dad's car."

Ricky said, "Look, there is a little light ahead."

Tom said, "I see Eddie and Dave and Sergeant Collins."

Ricky's dad called, "Are we glad to see you!"

Tom and Ricky told everyone about the mine and the gold they saw.

Sergeant Collins said, "We wanted to catch those men. They are wanted in other towns for salting mines with gold."

"Salting mines? What is that? You mean they put salt in a mine?" Tom asked.

Sergeant Collins said, "They put gold dust in a gun. Then they shoot the gun at the rocks in the mine. It looks like the rocks hold gold."

"But why?" Tom asked.

"I think I know. I bet those men just go where there are old gold mines. Is that right, Sergeant Collins?" Ricky asked.

"That's right, Ricky," the Sergeant answered.

"Then they make it look like the rocks still have lots of gold left in them," Ricky said.

"Why would they do that? What's this all about?" Tom asked.

"Then they bring people to the mine. They tell them that the mine is full of gold. They show them the gold all over the walls of the mine. Then they get the people to pay them a lot of money. The people think there is lots and lots of gold," Ricky said.

"I see what your're saying. Then, when they get the money, they leave town," Tom said.

"That's right. That's what's called salting a mine," Sergeant Collins said.

"How did you know where we were?" Ricky asked.

Eddie said, "Dave and I were late. We saw your bikes by the creek. We looked all over for you. Then we saw the truck by the hill. We knew we'd better call Sergeant Collins."

"Boy, are we glad you did that," Ricky said.

"Well, I'm going to call for more police. Those men have to come out of that cave one way or the other. We'll catch them this time," Sergeant Collins said.

All of a sudden Patches started to bark.

Ricky shined his flashlight on Patches.

"Look! Patches is all yellow," Eddie said.

"It's gold! Patches sat on the gold. He's full of gold dust from the cave. Patches! Don't move! Stay still," Ricky said.

Patches barked again. Then he ran right over to the creek and jumped in it.

"Oh, no!" Ricky yelled.

"He's washing all the gold off," Tom said.

"Come on, boys. Get your bikes. We'll all go back home," Ricky's dad said.

Patches came out of the water. He shook the water off him.

"We're going, too," Dave said.

"Come on over tomorrow. We'll tell you all about the tunnels," Ricky called out to Dave and Eddie.

"Tunnels?" Eddie called back.

"That's right," Ricky yelled.

"I don't want to know about tunnels. I want to know about gold," Eddie yelled.

"Well, if you find any we just might give you the mining rights," Ricky yelled.